citizens are

what they ar

— Plato

The city is

what it is

because its

citizens are

what they ar

— Plato

The city is

what it is

because its

citizens are

what they ar

— Plato

The city is

what it is

because its

citizens are

what they ar

— Plato

The city is

what it is

The city is
what it is
because its
citizens are
what they are
— Plato
The city is
what it is
because its
citizens are
what they are
— Plato
The city is
what it is
because its
citizens are
what they are
— Plato
The city is
what it is
because its
citizens are
what they are
— Plato
The city is
what it is

CALCUTTA

Repossessing the City

Leena Kejriwal

Foreword by Alka Saraogi. Essay by Dr. Tapati Guha Thakurta
Edited by Bina Sarkar Ellias

OM
Om Books International

This edition is published in 2007 by Om Books International, 4379/4B, Prakash House, Ansari Road, Daryaganj, New Delhi 110002, India

Tel: 91 11 23263363 . Fax: 91 11 23278091 . Email: sales@ombooks.com . Web: www.ombooks.com . ISBN 13: 978-81-87-87107-62-0, ISBN 10: 81-87107-62-6

Photographs copyright © Leena Kejriwal. Essay titled, "The Photographed City" copyright © Dr.Tapati Guha Thakurta

Editing and design: Bina Sarkar Ellias, Gallerie, Bombay . Processed, printed and bound in India by Thomson Press India Ltd.

For Ravi, Tushar and Vasvi

What I like about cities is that everything is king size, the beauty and the ugliness. —Joseph Brodsky, Russian-born American poet..

· FOREWORD ·

Alka Saraogi

It is an impossible mission to capture the essence or wholeness of Calcutta alias Kolkata, as the present city is called now, to correct the English mispronunciation of its original name. But this is a mission that ties me and Leena Kejriwal together via the different avenues of words and images. It all began when Leena asked me to accompany her at dawn one day to shoot the river Ganga from Howrah Bridge to Princep Ghat, for the cover picture of my first novel, *Kalikatha via Bypass* in 1997. Not having read my book, she had only partially grasped the multi-layered narrative from me. She must have been struck by the fascination the early Marwari migrants from the arid desert of Rajasthan had for the holy river, and a city whose streets were washed every morning by its water.

We ultimately settled for the monument of James Princep that had been erected to welcome King Edward VII from England in the year 1843 A. D. The yellow monument, with its stately pillars near the river, had remained in my childhood memories. I vainly tried to locate it whenever I passed by, without realising that the whole area had been cordoned off for years by tin sheets for the second river bridge. A rusted tin sheet had recently fallen off to show us a glimpse of the monument, usurped by an overgrown jungle.

It was history, impressive and elegant, eaten up by the decay and indifference of the present. Forgotten are our values for freedom fighters and the early austere lifestyle of the Marwaris. By the year 1997, India celebrated its 50 years of independence with much pomp, while 50 per cent of its population still languished below the poverty line. If this seems like a digression in my foreword, it is only so, because as fifth-generation members of the Marwari diaspora in Calcutta, both Leena and I have this preoccupation with the physical and emotional transitions that the spaces and neighbourhoods as well as the people and communities of Calcutta have gone through in the last decades.

It makes Calcutta what it is today, a complex, undecipherable amalgam of modernity and oldness, human warmth and apathy, rickshaws, trams and limousines, the fish and vegetable markets and newly mushrooming malls, the Kali worshippers and the omnipresent prostitutes in nearby red-light areas, the various jostling, overcrowded *mohallas* (neighbourhoods) of different communities with graffiti on the walls and the green unhindered expanse from Chowringhee to the flowing Hooghly, the skyline dotted with multistoried structures along with the dwarfed colonial buildings, College Street bookshops and the rampant child labour at the roadside tea stalls, thousands of pavement dwellers and the middleclass Bengali *babus* with their well-preserved dignity.

You will find different Calcuttas through Leena's camera here: the Calcutta of the barefoot rickshaw-puller, the Calcutta of intellectuals debating at the Coffee House, the Calcutta of porters carrying more weight than their own, the Calcutta of idol makers, of devotees and deities of the Kali temples in the city, the Calcutta of mosque, and synagogue and church, the Calcutta of beggars and prostitutes, the Calcutta of *zamindars'* palaces in the North and the Calcutta of the unfathomable and unacknowledged protagonist of this book — the irrepressible human spirit in timeless time.

· THE PHOTOGRAPHED CITY ·

Dr. Tapati Guha Thakurta

I.

The city has had a long and contentious relationship with the art of photography. Aerial panoramas from atop the Ochterlony monument to close-up details of slums and pavement life, from architectural invocations of the imperial capital to the obsessive imaging of the squalor and congestion of the post-colonial metropolis, there has been a continuous outpouring of images of Calcutta, from the latter half of the 19th century into the present. Over time, these photographs can be seen to perform different functions for different viewers, featuring under the colonial genre of 'Views of Calcutta' and the latter-day genres of 'news', 'documentary' or 'art' photography. The process of the production of such a photographic image-pool on the city has, however, inevitably been fraught with tensions and disaffections. Impressive as it is in its range and volume, the legacy of Calcutta's photographic images has always had to fight a festering unease — a discomfort at the ways in which spaces and lives have been framed, and a resistance to certain dominant stereotypes about the city that have been produced and naturalised by photography.

For generations now, Calcuttans have recoiled at the main photographic constructions of the colonial and post-colonial city. If Calcutta's image as the 'City of Palaces' fast lost its currency in the years after Independence, the images that most powerfully replaced it in the international media have been a cause of even greater consternation. During the 1960s and 70s, photography invoked (in ways no textual description ever could) the all-pervasive image of the 'City of Joy', represented by unspeakable destitution and human degradation, and the saviour figure of Mother Teresa, even as it relentlessly replayed Rudyard Kipling's proverbial image of the "chance-erected, chance-directed... packed and pestilential town", over which death has never ceased to look down. Those who found these images insulting and objectionable were, of course, the city's intellectuals and middle classes — they were the ones who actively questioned their conspicuous exclusion from this standard photographic corpus and wished to re-image the city from their own point of view; and it is their interventions that brought into the field an alternative set of representational idioms that sought to challenge or bypass these image stereotypes.

What such struggles over representation underscore are a vortex of larger debates as to who and what should be the fit subjects of photography, and what should be the best modes of their portrayal. On whose terms could one arrive at a more representative, non-derogatory, yet at the same time, non-falsified series of images of Calcutta? In what ways can photography represent without objectifying, or render subjects aesthetic without detracting from their realism and their authenticity? How can a photographer negotiate for her or himself the position of a sensitive 'insider' and view the city from within? And, most crucially, can one take the liberty of photographing places and peoples, objects and scenes, without having to capture the 'essence' and the 'true spirit' of the city? The burden of authenticity, representative coverage and correct portrayal, one can argue, has been the bane of the medium— a burden that even the certified practices of art photography cannot shirk off. This burden and these questions, today, must be confronted upfront by any photographer who wishes to produce one more set of representations of the city. They are particularly crucial to the self-positioning of Leena Kejriwal, who has lived and grown in the city, fine-tuned her professional skills within city circles, and has kept rediscovering her known city through her camera lenses. Before we turn to the course and content of her Calcutta photographs, let us briefly consider the lay of the vast field before her, and see how her work may be situated within it.

II.

A key problem that I would like to explore, in this section, is the continuous dichotomy and interplay of 'outsider' and 'insider' perspectives in the history of this genre of city photographs. This history is as old as the technology itself: it takes off with the very arrival of photography in British India in the middle decades of the 19th century, and moves almost concomitantly with the first experiments and advances in the technology in Europe. Calcutta became one of the founding sites for the development and refinement of the fledgling medium in India, and for the production of its earliest repertoire of images. As early as the 1850s and 60s, we have British pioneers turning their lenses on the grand vistas, mansions and river front of this 'first city of the empire' to experiment with the new techniques of hand-coloured salt prints, the collotype, the wet-collodion or the albumen print process. More than any other Indian metropolis, Calcutta emerged as the favoured subject of imperial photography, providing it with its exemplary images of the 'urban picturesque'— the 'white town' with its towering spires, columned arcades, and neo-classical facades, set off by broad expanses of sky and road fronts, and tiny figures of natives and local street life, with occasional glimpses of the bazaar and hutments of the 'black town' providing a perfect contrast. The pictorial model developed by the engravings of Thomas and William Daniell and James Baillie Fraser and the lithographs of Charles D'Oyly was strategically lifted on to photography in the earliest city albums of Bourne and Shepherd.

In the same years, Calcutta also saw the rise of a flourishing indigenous practice of photography, marked by the setting up of independent photographic societies and commercial studios and the careers of a significant number of Bengalis in the field. As with their Parsi equivalents in Bombay and many of the Indian royalty and aristocracy who developed a passion for the new medium, local photographers in Calcutta focused their practice largely on the art of portrait photography. Bengali studios quickly developed the fine art of studio portraiture, with elaborate props and painted backgrounds and carefully choreographed postures and costumes, fashioning cabinet-card, individual and family portraits for a growing clientele. Some of these studios also advertised their expertise in outdoor photography of ceremonies, public events, parties and *shikars*. The genre of city-views seemed to have seldom featured within either their commercial or their non-commercial repertoire. While photography served as an ideal aid in the fashioning of new elite and middleclass identities, it did not elicit the same compulsions towards an architectural and ethnographic imaging of the urban spaces of modern India. The latter remained largely a European monopoly and prerogative till well into the 20th century. The worlds one most closely inhabits, as we know, are often the ones that are most difficult to document or commemorate. Caught up in an everlasting nostalgia for the lost worlds of the village, the city would hardly configure in the literary, artistic or even the photographic imagination of the Bengali *bhadralok*.

It is from the middle of the 20th century that one can track several distinct shifts in these trends. The break registers itself most dramatically in the decades after Independence in a new wave of international media coverage of Calcutta as the archetypal Third World metropolis, embodying, as it was proclaimed, "the worst of urban disasters". The British themselves had long despaired over the fate of a city that had grown helter-skelter out of a swamp, and had struggled to impose civic order, discipline and sanitation on a Calcutta that was perennially ridden with poverty and pestilence. The underside of the city of promenades and sprawling greens, of grand government buildings and private mansions, had always been the chaos and congestion of the native quarters. The problems of the 'black town' threatened to continuously spill over the fragile boundaries that separated it from the 'white town'. It was hardly surprising then that, with the final end of British rule, the city was seen to slip into what writers have termed an irredeemable "morass of third-worldness". Through the 1950s and into the 70s, it was once again, photography (especially the spreading genres of news and documentary photography) that worked most powerfully at serving up Calcutta's "wretched of the earth" before the donor agencies and the moral conscience of a post-colonial world.

Yet, the same city in the same years would also nurture a variety of other contrasting photographic narratives. Produced from within Calcutta, these showcased urban growth and development, the fashionable 'high-life' of the city's clubs, hotels and restaurants, and the animated public spaces and intellectual culture of a city that clung proudly to its image as the 'cultural capital' of India. By the 1940s, the city's veteran professional photographer, Ahmed Ali, had begun operating out of his studio in Palace Court on Kyd Street, feeding the period's new demands of advertising, industrial and commercial photography, producing his voluminous archive of images of an unfailingly glamorous and resplendent city. Over the next two decades, Ahmed Ali's photographs provide riveting profiles of the Telephone Bhavan under construction, the New Market lit up for Christmas, the still meticulously preserved buildings of Martin Burn and the Army and Navy Stores, the Lighthouse Cinema packed to capacity, or a cabaret at the Princess Bar at Grand Hotel. And he juxtaposes these with equally compelling images of the more plebian city, of double-decker buses, commuters at Sealdah station and football crowds at the Maidan.

These were the years that also saw the emergence in the city of a new breed of intellectual photographers, both amateur and professional—figures like Parimal Goswami or Kamakshi Prasad Chattopadhyay—who turned their gaze closely on their own literary and artistic milieu. Introducing us to Calcutta's celebrated circles of writers, poets, artists, singers and actors, these photographs also take us into historic mass public events like the 1955 reception of the Soviet leaders, Bulganin and Krushchev, at the Brigade Parade Grounds. It is this line of photography that would beget the more specialised genres of theatre and cinema stills of several talented photographers of the subsequent decades, not least among them, Nemai Ghosh, whose career peaked to fame on the sets of Satyajit Ray's films. It is also from this widening corpus of images that we have from this period another familiar iconography of the 'intellectual' and 'political' city. This is an iconography which produced its canon of archetypal images of the Coffee House *adda*, of student canteens and booksellers on College Street, of street walls filled with political graffiti, or of spectacular crowds at rallies at the Shahid Minar and the Brigade Parade Grounds.

The twin métiers of 'art' and 'news' photography evolved as closely overlapping spheres over this period, producing a genre of city images that effectively blended the demands of both aesthetics and accurate documentation. Some of the finest examples of such a blend can be seen in the works of Shambhu Shaha, another of Calcutta's veteran freelance photographers of the immediately pre and post-Independence years. What is particularly instructive is the way photographers like Shambhu Shaha, along with several photojournalists of his generation, compellingly return our attention to the 'man on the street', to the everyday slum and pavement life of the city. Far from being erased or swept under covers, the poor and ordinary folk of Calcutta acquire an iconic presence in the city photographs of this time — in images of people wading waist-deep in water-logged streets, of queues and fights at roadside hydrants, of cooking on pavements, and most pointedly, in the close-ups of the haunted faces of the refugees of 1971. These photographs provide the most jolting reminder of the two massive lots of refugee influxes from East Pakistan and Bangladesh that pushed the dislocation and poverty of the city to bursting point, and cast Calcutta's image in one more mould: that of the volatile refugee city.

In the 1970s, these multiple strands of images came together in the production of one of the first of a new genre of plush 'coffee-table' albums on Calcutta, with photographs by Raghubir Singh. It carried text by *The New York Times* correspondent, Joseph Lelyveld, that typified the passion and empathy, and, no less, the trauma and sense of assault that Calcutta produced in a foreigner. And it presented a spread of images, which in their range and intensity, constituted what became (and still remains) the most seductive canon of photographic representations of the city. We have here Raghubir Singh's panoramic shots of a traffic-clogged Harrison Road leading to the Howrah Bridge and his aerial views of a sea of figures, assembled for Sheikh Mujibur Rahman's rally at the Maidan. We have also intimate, face-to-face contact with *thelawallahs* and rickshaw pullers, vegetable and fish vendors, beggars and ragpickers, inmates of Mother Teresa's "Nirmal Hriday", wrestlers at the Hooghly, idol makers at Kumartuli, clerks at Writers' Building, stockbrokers in their cubicles at India Exchange Place, and slogan-shouting activists of the Youth Congress. This rich ethnography of the peoples of Calcutta then meanders into middle class homes, pastimes and festivities, and lovingly lingers on the all-time favourite scene of women smearing each other with *sindur* to bid farewell to Goddess Durga. And it also offers privileged entry into the lives of the city's rich and fading aristocrats (where we see polo and horse-racing at the Turf Club and a carriage standing before the Marble Palace of the Mullicks), and into another kind of exclusive artistic space (where we encounter the now-deceased Satyajit Ray on his film set, or Jamini Roy in his studio, surrounded by his paintings).

If Raghubir Singh's images held their ground as the period's most prestigious and marketable invocations of Calcutta, they did not stem the flow of other modes of photographic engagements with the city. One could cite here, the example of a photo-documentation project on the 'People of Calcutta', undertaken in the 1970s by a group of young photographers under the aegis of a Jesuit audio-visual media organisation called Chitrabani. Consciously 'alternative' in its self-image, shying away from the press and advertising media, the project grappled with the idea of a counter practice of non-commercial, socially committed documentary photography, where the prime intention was to use photography to give a face and identity to the poor of the city. As Chitrabani's founding director, Father Gaston Roberge stated, theirs was a new experimentation in deploying photography towards transforming the lives of those whose images it garnered. Whether or not it ever fulfilled such a vision of 'ethical praxis of documentary photography', what such a project did achieve, was the production of a large archive of images on slum housing and living conditions, on the variety of trades, skills and occupations that make up the city's fringe economy, or on the diverse forms of transport, street entertainment and wall graffiti that were all quintessentially Calcuttan. Photography, here, can be seen to have geared itself to the detailed needs of visual ethnography and social documentation.

Yet, in such cases too, the lines of distinction between 'art' and 'ethnography', between aesthetic framing and authentic recording, become impossible to discern. Stripped of their altruistic intentions and moral platitudes, the Chitrabani photographs seem to easily merge with the larger photographic iconography of the popular life and culture of Calcutta that was already in wide circulation. For all the intimate scrutiny of the camera, the toiling rickshaw puller, the sleeping vendor or the child in the slum never become individuals in these photographs — they remain, as always, specimens and types, embodying in their anonymity the supposedly 'true' character of the city. The point at issue here concerns the very art of photography and the kinds of images of Calcutta it has nurtured and authorised. There was clearly, by now, a well-honed language and vocabulary of city photography that was firmly in place, that tended to inadvertently encompass this whole range of scenes and subjects within its representational frames. Photography, we could argue, had become a powerful self-referential system of citations, in which the city would continually reproduce itself through a recognisable trajectory of image constructions. Does the field, then, foreclose all possibilities of breaking out of these moulds and creating a sharply different image repertoire? Is there at all a new compulsion to the choices of subjects, spaces and images through which Calcutta may now be represented in photographs?

III

Such questions become pertinent as we turn, in this last section, to the particular modes of Leena Kejriwal's photographic engagement with the city. My purpose in laying out this long, earlier history of city photography has been to underline the power and appeal of this lineage, and to address the ways in which her work demands to be placed within it. Over several decades, now, we have seen how the city has been actively reclaimed and reimaged by Calcutta's own groups of photographers. Leena Kejriwal can be seen to closely belong to this history, spinning out a continuing thread of an intimate 'insider' vision of the city's peoples and spaces. But, as we draw out the links and continuities with this past history, we must also pitch her work within a new 'present' — and ask in what ways it speaks to changing times and how it visualises the current life and character of the city.

Calcutta is today a city swept by change. The rapidity and scale of this transformation is astounding, as much for those of us who live here and find ourselves daily confronted by its effects, as for anybody visiting the city after a gap of a few years or even months. This transformation has had its particularly startling repercussions in a city where for so long nothing seemed to ever proceed or progress. Then suddenly, in the course of the late 1990s and 2000s, a long delayed tide of change came crashing into Calcutta — razing old structures and neighbourhoods, building flyover after flyover, shopping mall after shopping mall, allowing a new spate of luxurious, gated apartment complexes to mushroom in all parts of the city. Two decades ago, the newest features of Calcutta would have been the underground metro, carved out of the bowels of the city after years of overground dislocation, to miraculously connect the two extreme ends of Dumdum and Tollygunge — or the bypass which opened up the eastern wetland fringes and became one of the city's first multi-lane, fast-moving highways, linking Park Street and Gariahat with Ultadanga and the airport road. Also still relatively new would have been the rapidly expanding elite township of Salt Lake on the northeast end of the bypass, where (as many Calcuttans complained) one repeatedly lost one's bearings in a maze of roundabouts and road grids. Now, the novelty of all these pales before the super edifice of the Lower Circular Road flyover that transports one in a flash from Park Circus to the Victoria Memorial, bobbing over the heads of old familiar buildings — or before the mega New Town of Rajarhat and the sprawling IT city on Sector V of Salt Lake that have sprouted out of nowhere as the city's latest hubs of residence and office life. The greatest invasion has been of hotels and high-rise apartment blocks, along the full stretch of the bypass, as also of ever new malls, multiplexes, coffee shops, restaurants and exclusive schools, with giant, glittering billboards advertising them.

It is in the context of these dramatic transformations in Calcutta's topography and lifestyles that the photographs we have discussed acquire a special nostalgic and historical resonance. They remind us, for instance, of the famous Firpos market, whose last remnants were burnt to cinders a few years ago, or of New Market in its heyday, now pushed to near extinction by the construction of new shopping marts and parking lots. The realisation also dawns that double-decker buses have altogether gone, that the current buses no longer have commuters precariously spilling out of their doors, as was once so typical of Calcutta, and that even the city's trademark hand-pulled rickshaws are now to be seen only in a shrinking space of the old city, increasingly replaced by cycle and auto-rickshaws throughout the greater metropolitan area. The beggars and pavement dwellers that once dominated the image of the city are today rendered more and more invisible by the new shining facades and structures that are overtaking the streets. And, in the latest projection of a new civic spirit and culture, even Calcutta's notorious political graffiti and traffic-stopping rallies are now things of the past.

This sense of change, today, is inescapable and overpowering. Yet, what is also remarkable is the way it remains conspicuously occluded and sidelined within a continuing genre of city photographs. The reasons for this are not hard to find. It lies in the constant compulsions of this genre of photography to produce images that are 'timeless' and reflective of the 'true essence' of the city. As the new city gets sucked into the soulless homogeneity of affluence and consumerism — as every high-rise and mega store replicates its type with a predictable uniformity — the photographer is driven even more to hold on to all that is still unique, quirky and distinctive about Calcutta, and to seek out the vestiges of what lingers and survives. Photography can be seen to take on a self-assigned role of remembrance, recuperation and salvage, in turning its back resolutely on the spaces of transformation and the spectacle of change. As we go through Leena Kejriwal's photographs of Calcutta, we see how such a charge of recovering an 'old' Calcutta unfolds itself in all its detail and depth, how she subtly excavates the past in the present, and in the process presents a very different ethnography of the contemporary city.

The book begins with resonant mist-laden views of the river far up north, moving up and down its banks from a temple on the Baranagar ghat to fishing boats and nets on the stretch between Baghbazar and Posta, that was once the village of Sutanuti. It thus takes us back to the founding histories of the city that would spring out of the three villages — Sutanuti, Gobindapur and Kalikata — and the first trading settlements and fortifications of the East India Company along the Hooghly. It then lays out a topography of the city that runs largely along the traditional pilgrim route from the Chitteswari Temple on the northernmost tip of Chitpur Road to the vicinities around the Kalighat temple in the south. The choice of these two temples, both of whose histories go back in legend well beyond the time of British Calcutta and both of which produce a special sacred mythology of the city, are important not only in defining the territorial belt of the 'traditional' old city. They also pinpoint the photographer's particular fascination with the closely integrated worlds of devotion, ritual, trade and commerce that typify the neighbourhoods of Chitpur and Kalighat, and mark out the special character of the public life of this broad area.

Recurrent motifs in these photographs are of temples, mosques and sites of worship. Journeying through Chitpur Road, we are taken from the Chitteswari and Siddheswari Kali temples (the latter, with its historic location opposite the 'Black Pagoda' of Raja Govindrama Mitra) to the Nakhoda Masjid, and then made to meander through several spots for worship on the ghats along the Hooghly into the dark interiors of the Durgeshwari Shibmandir off a bylane of Nimtala. The tour continues through the Firangi Kali temple on Bowbazar, and then wanders far south and west, to hover around the temple and alleys of Kalighat, to wander through the mosque and graveyard of the exiled family of Tipu Sultan at the Tollygunge-Anwar Shah Road crossing, and to offer a spectacular interior view of Wajid Ali Shah's Imambara at Metiabruz. From the exterior facades, the camera penetrates deep into the inner temple sanctums, or zooms from above into the resplendent interior chambers and courtyards of the Nakhoda Masjid and the Metiabruz Imambara. Leena Kejriwal's loving focus is always on peoples and objects within these spaces — as she intimately profiles the Chitteswari deity, the dark giant *linga* rising almost invisibly inside the Nimtala Mandir, the *pujaris* at Siddheswari and the Firangi Kali temple, and a little *burkha*-clad girl at a Chitpur *madrassa*; or she lets her camera sweep down on a view of a devotee collapsed on the floor of the Imambara at Metiabruz. Once in a while, the objects alone take centre stage — as with piles of red medicinal boxes inscribed in Urdu maintained by the Hakim of the Imambara. Leena's photographic engagement with ritual and worship also takes her into the institutions and practices of Calcutta's diverse religious and ethnic communities — into the Fire Temple of the Parsis on Metcalf Street, into a service at the Armenian Holy Church of Nazareth on Armenian Street, or into a Bihari Chhat Puja procession on its way to Babughat. And it also leads her into the private puja rooms of traditional north Calcutta Bengali homes, where she participates in the evening *kirtan* and *arati*, or in the daily commemoration of the death-bed and personal belongings of a family patriarch.

A parallel preoccupation that pervades this book are with the markets, wholesale markets and quaint little shops that are encountered throughout the stretch of north, central and south Calcutta. Old markets, once the lifeline of the city's economy, remain a quintessential feature of the trading and commercial networks that sustain large sections of Calcutta's population. Here, the tour trundles through the wholesale potato, onion, fruit and cotton marts of Posta and Machhua, off Chitpur Road, into the stalls of the fish and vegetable vendors of the Sreemani Market at Manicktala, down to the Saagbazar at Sealdah. In each market, what captivates the photographer is the play of darkness and light, the bustle of activity contrasted by the order and neatness of the wares on sale, whether they are sacks of potatoes, piles of bananas to be auctioned, or silvery rows of large and small fish. What equally magnetises our attention are the people who animate these markets — the fish seller who weighs his fish against a vibrant Kali, painted on the walls of his stall, the *babu* in his white *fatua* and *dhoti* who haggles with the vegetable vendor, or the elderly widow who scrutinises every potato she buys. These are also spaces that can amply indulge the photographer's fascination with objects and displays — as is evident in her detailing of the calendar art that fills the walls of these shops and stalls, of all the different items (dominated by an antique, carved wooden cupboard with mirrors) in the meticulously arranged space of a Burrabazar *gaddi*, or of the rows of glass bottles of *attar* and *zarda* that line the nearly hundred-year-old premises of the Gupta Perfumery in Shyambazar. The tour of markets and little shops moves from north Calcutta to other far-flung areas in the centre and the south. We are taken, for instance, into the Chinese food market that is set up every Sunday morning on the streets of the old Tiretty market, into a second-hand book and record shop on Elliot Street, into the evening lights and the Christmas decoration stalls outside New Market and into the city's oldest cake shop, Nahoum's confectionery, inside the market. We also travel south to Bhawanipur and Kalighat, where we see the ritual opening of new account books by Bengali shopkeepers on *Poila Baisakh* (the Bengali new year day). All along, there is a search for the derelict and the archaic that continue to linger in these spaces— as with the watch repairer in his shop on Amherst Street, the wizened old tailor who sits at a first-floor barred window on a Kalighat street, and the empty, dilapidated doctors' clinics on Bowbazar Street.

There are several other thematic strands that can be drawn out of this collection of city photographs. There is, for instance, a close imaging of some key neighbourhoods of the city through an unusual focus on objects, peoples and scenes that subtly encode their identities. It is hardly surprising that Leena Kejriwal turns to some of Calcutta's most famous old neighbourhoods, like Chitpur, Kalighat or Bhawanipur. What is new is the way she invokes a feel of Chitpur through details of wrought-iron balustrades, crumbling housefronts and old markets— of Kalighat through figures of old women squatting outside the temple and a motif of a bright green sari hanging outside the tenement of the red-light quarters — and of a woman looking out of a window through festoons of red flags of the CPI(M), and eye-catching wall graffiti of football heroes, that locate us squarely in the time of this year's assembly election and World Cup fever in the city. Other familiar spaces on the cityscape are reinscribed here through a more conventional image series. The Maidan is seen here through a canopy of trees, flanked by distant views of the Victoria Memorial and the high-rises on Chowringhee. There is a long sojourn into the famous idol-making quarters of Kumartuli, up north beyond Baghbazar. A perennial favourite of Calcutta photographers, Kumartuli's bylanes and semi-finished clay idols of Durga and Kali have long reigned as the most canonical images of the city. We see Leena Kejriwal elaborating this canon, with dramatic angles and splintered frames, and a series of close-ups of enlarged clay torsos and ornamental panels that seem to grow autonomously, regardless of their surroundings. In keeping with her signatorial style, Kumartuli as a place is captured through a myriad objects, fragments and details.

The point that needs emphasis is the way this corpus of photographs continually acts upon the familiar and the conventional— the way these activate not only the image of the 'old' city, but also an older legacy of subjects and motifs, to strategically insert these within a new present. So, some of Calcutta's best known colonial monuments reappear here in contemporary frames of decay or restoration — the forlorn steeple of St. John's Church, now overgrown with vegetation, juxtaposed with the renovated and illuminated Palladian colonnades of Princep Ghat, now made to host evening music concerts. The 'great houses' of north Calcutta — the *zamindari* mansions of the Tagores of Pathuriaghata and Jorasanko, the Debs of Shobabazar, or the Lahas of College Street also make their routine appearance, in shifting registers of nostalgia and requiem. Often, we find a single image of dereliction — of clothes strung across the now barely recognisable Scottish turrets of the Tagore Castle on Prasanna Coomar Tagore Street — resonating more powerfully than the sumptuous scenes of Durga Puja celebrations in the *thakur dalan* of Shobhabazar. Also present in the volume are Calcutta's famous coffee houses and cabins as the most representative symbols of public intellectual life and *addas* of the older city. But the very manner of photography now implicitly casts them as curious relics of a bygone era — as we see with the distanced, top-angle view of the dangling fans and liveried bearers of the Prince Albert Hall Coffee House, or with the old man absorbed in his newspaper at the Favourite Cabin on Beadon Street, a place that was once the meeting point of the revolutionary terrorists of the Swadeshi years.

Nowhere is the seductive draw of the existing lineage of imagery more apparent than in the book's profiling of Calcutta's peoples and communities. Yet, we also see how this rich ethnography of the city's characteristic trades, occupations and social types periodically runs against the grain, interjecting sudden doses of warmth and humour into subjects, or distilling new subjectivities where one least expects them. While the archetypal Bengali housewives (in their gold jewellery and red-bordered white saris) hold their fort at the Durga Puja festivities in aristocratic north Calcutta homes, the person who steals the show is a little old lady on the streets of Kalighat, who gingerly reaches out for an afternoon snack of *telebhaja*, or batter-fried savouries. A rickshaw puller pans by, carrying an idol of Saraswati, his figure blurred in the movement of lights and speeding traffic. We are introduced to a variety of more unusual figures — like the milk and *malai* seller from Rajasthan in his shop at Chitpur, the doctor advertising treatment for eczema in a run-down Bowbazar clinic, and a *Bahurupee* dressed as Kali striding down Lake Market, as a rare remnant of the long disappeared folk cultures of the city.

The book also reaches out to the now vanishing communities of Armenians, Jews, Chinese and Parsis who were the first to have given Calcutta her historically cosmopolitan character. What is again remarkable is the photographer's imaginative culling of subjects, spaces and scenes that can synoptically represent each of these tight-knit ethnic groups. So, for the Armenians, she offers a view of a family drawing room full of interesting people, and a peep through an ornate grill into a service at the Armenian church. For the Anglo-Indians, the scene of an intimate birthday celebration with three generations of a family; for the Chinese, a camaraderie of men congregating at a club in the old Chinatown at Bowbazar; for the Jews, the solitary figure of Mr. Nahoum still proudly selling his confectionery at his New Market shop; and for the Parsis, a cluster of elderly figures alighting from a rickshaw at the Fire Temple. Such ethnographies, as we have seen, lavish the same order of attention also on Bengali aristocratic and middleclass homes, and end up encompassing the photographer's own community of Marwari women, who are shown at a family wedding, one of whom, Rita Dalmiya, is later singled out as a lady of special educational distinction.

It is out of this pageantry of characters and communities that we arrive at the book's final round of photographs of individual personalities of the city — among them, Calcutta's seniormost octogenarian painter, Paritosh Sen, theatre director Gautam Haldar, the antiquarian scholar and tour guide, Shantimoy Bhattacharya posing next to his family altar; Lady Sheila Mukherjee, a daughter of the Lord Sinha family, and the city's most eminent cultural patrons, Aveek and Rakhi Sarkar. Each is shown in the specific milieu of their residence, with fine furniture and precious objects — reflecting their individual personalities.

Yet, the photographer's tryst with the rich and famous is brief. All along, the more compelling draw of the book is towards the humbler, everyday world of streets and markets, towards the ageing, the frail and archaic that tenaciously live out their lives under the bulldozers of change and development. Leena Kejriwal's forte lies in repeatedly seeking out the ordinary and the uneventful, and in delving into the minutiae of objects, surroundings, expressions and demeanours, to create resonant images out of the most innocuous of alleys, the messiest of markets or the most unexceptional figure on the street. As an image maker, she brings to bear on her spaces and subjects the combined art of the miniaturist and the still life painter. We see this, for instance, in the way she lavishes attention on the folds and borders of a sari fluttering outside a door, in her obsession with every small object in altars, puja rooms, shops and streets, or in the manner in which she treats sacks of onions or rows of bottles with the same attention to detail as she does an ornate bedstead or an antique cupboard. This is how she enters from deep within and intimately inhabits every scene she photographs. And this, I would say, becomes the pith of her private 'insider' engagement with her city. The Calcutta that is held together in this volume of photographs is one that is intensely her own — discovered through every old neighbourhood she roamed, claimed and reconstituted — and given its niche within the long lineage of city photography.

· CALCUTTA: REPOSSESSING THE CITY ·

Leena Kejriwal

Calcutta or Kolkata as it is now called, is for me a city that has grown into a world, and the world has opened new windows to my understanding of its teeming life and people. Born and raised in a traditional family, my growing years here were sheltered from the hustle-bustle of the city's life. It was, interestingly, a British couple, Mr and Mrs Horsman, family friends who stayed with us, who really opened my eyes to the city— its architecture, colonial past and culture. I began to see it with new eyes and the urge to capture its essence became a need. A short course in photography initiated me into the exciting possibilities of the camera as a medium to express myself. Thus, armed with technical knowledge, I embarked on an exciting journey to mirror my viewfinder's discoveries.

It was a revelation! My myopic vision had given way to a broader perspective of the vibrant city I live in. What came as a surprise was the simple beauty of life on the street. There was an innate grace in the midst of chaos. Humble spaces, like tea shops with their gods and goddesses, yellow lemons and green chillies in marketplaces, a touch of red hibiscus offered to a kitschy image of Kali, soon began appearing in my growing canvas. My explorations took me from the northern end of the city, near Kumartuli, towards Kalighat in the South, through various spaces and phases of its meandering history. It was, however, the able guidance of Dr. Tapati Guha Thakurta that helped me structure the images into "Neighbourhood and Spaces", and "People and Communities".

The Bichuli Ghat at Sutanuti, close to where Job Charnock had supposedly landed with a huge iron post to anchor his ship, stands testimony to the history of Calcutta and how it came into being. Spaces such as these, lingering with history, evoked a sense of nostalgia and led me further into lanes and bylanes. In these, I discovered old market spaces, each with its own distinctive colour and flavour. The deep pink of Posta, the old yellow-green tiles of Shreemani, the black Bahurupia at the Lake Market, the blue Shyama Kali painted on the walls of the fish market, all left an impression on my imagination and lured me deeper into the lives of the people of the city.

There was Shantimoyda, my guide, who helped me explore the city and its textures. He, with his treasure house of knowledge, is representative of the fading ethos of the Bengali renaissance. The majority of the populace is Bengali, followed by the Marwaris and Biharis. The smaller communities are as much a part of the city. I found a yuppie set of Anglo Indians hosting a beyblade competition at the Rangers Club, Parsis at their fire temple, the Armenians at a school where they spoke Persian, and the Chinese at the Tiretty market which is a hub for their community. The city probably had a much more cosmopolitan flavour in the past than it has now. It has been home to many communities such as the Jews, Greeks, Danes, and of course, the British, since times when it was a major trading centre of the East. And each of these has left their mark on the city, adding to its history, architecture, cuisine and flavour.

Calcutta continues to evolve, gathering new layers. It straddles its two worlds, the old and the new, with an innate, quirky resilience. As a photographer, it never fails to fascinate me and every time I am on the road, it reveals yet another facet, another lane to explore and capture.

From Chitteshwari to Kalighat, the dotted path traces the route I travelled from the northern end of the city to the southern — going through the 'native town' in areas like Chitpur through Dalhousie, the 'white town', which is still reminiscent of the Raj. And through its neighouring areas of New Market and Bhowanipur, which have their own stories to tell. And finally, across the Maidan to Kalighat.

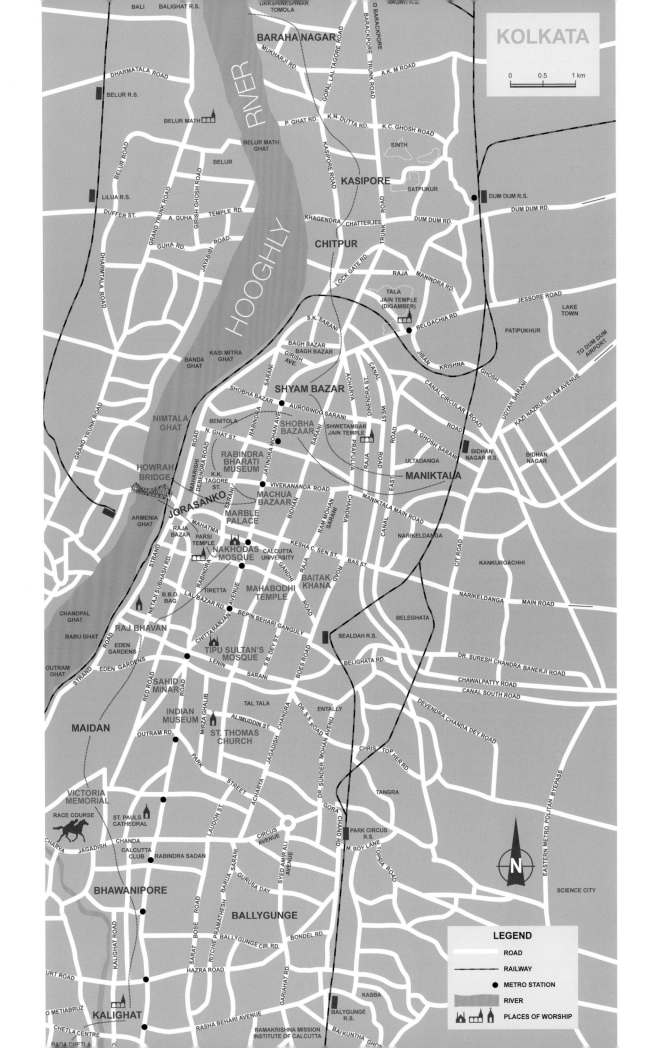

To sit in the dust of Calcutta is better than to grace the throne of another dominion. — Mirza Ghalib

Neighbourhoods and Spaces

The river Hooghly (Hugli) has given birth and life to the city, shaping the unique riverine character of the urban settlement that grew out of marshes, tidal creeks, mangrove swamps and wetlands. Its broad curve runs north to south, vertically mapping the city, separating Calcutta from Howrah, leading into the vast Gangetic Delta (the world's largest) in the Bay of Bengal. There was a time when the Hooghly was the crucial arterial route for all the trade in the region, sustaining a series of European commercial settlements along its banks. The name of the river in this stretch is linked to the town of Hooghly further up north, which, along with the seven villages of Saptagram (Satgaon), had flourished as a major Portuguese and Dutch trading depot during the 16th and 17th centuries. The river was then easily navigable by sea-going ships as far as the Adi-Ganga (what later came to be called Tolly's Nullah in Calcutta), from which point cargo would move in country boats to Satgaon and Hooghly. It was the silting of the river up north that pushed the seat of commerce south and made for the rise of the English trading settlement along the three villages of Gobindapur, Sutanuti and Kalikata, which, in turn, became the nucleus of the colonial city. Ever since, the fortunes of the river-dependent alluvial city have closely depended on the desilting and revitalisation of the Hooghly. Today, the river is crossed by small fishing boats and ferries that carry daily commuters between the shores.

Once the main lifeline of Calcutta and the key commercial thorough-fare of this trading belt, the Hooghly has long lost its importance as a shipping route to the world. The city in its more recent history has grown with its back to the river. In large stretches, as we see in this northern bend beyond the Chitpur Creek, it remains a sleepy meandering river with country boats trudging along.

Bichuli Ghat, in the stretch between Baghbazar and Posta, marks the old village of Sutanuti and the historic landing spot where the city's avowed 'founder', Job Charnock, first arrived in August 1690 in search of a commercial outpost for the East India Company. Traces of this history can still be seen in a huge metal knob used to anchor cargo boats to the shore.

The crumbling, but still impressive, precinct of this *pancha-ratna* (five-spired) temple, stands at the Baranagar Ghat. It is one of the first landmarks on the banks of the Hooghly as one comes down the river towards Calcutta. The area is said to have got its name from *varahas*, or wild boars, which once filled the jungle areas around this locality.

Chitpur was the vibrant religious, commercial and cultural heart of the 'Black Town', and still preserves the archetypal face of the traditional, unchanging city. With a history that pushes back well beyond the British founding of Calcutta, Chitpur Road is one of the oldest pilgrimage routes in this region, connecting the Chitteshwari temple in the north to the Kalighat temple in the south. Thickly forested and infested with thugs and bandits, this dangerous route was transformed during the 19th century into a major hub of artisanal crafts, shops and markets, and the earliest time of the Bengali print and publishing trade. It is off the many lanes mushrooming out of Chitpur, that one can see the settlement, for instance, of the *kumors*, clay potters and idolmakers, at Kumartuli; the *shankaris*, conch-shell workers at Shankaritola; the *kasais*, butchers at Kasaitola; the spice merchants at Beniatola; the fruit, vegetable and cotton wholesale retailers in the markets of Posta; and the cheap book and picture publishers at Bat-tala. It was said that one could buy anything, from a needle to an elephant, at Chitpur. Chitpur's reputation thrived as a microcosm of the many religions, occupations and communities that made for the truly cosmopolitan character of the city. Alongside the city's oldest temples and mosques, the vicinities became home to a medley of trading communities — upcountry Muslims, Marwaris, Armenians, Jews and Chinese — even as it stood at the vanguard of many of the 'great houses' of the Bengali aristocracy.

The Chitteshwari (a colloquial rendering of Chitreswari) temple stands at the northern end of Chitpur Road, where Chitpur leads on to the equally old quarters of Kashipur. The legends surrounding this temple go back far beyond the time of the British. They tell us of an idol of goddess Durga, which a notorious bandit of this region, Chitey Dakat, constructed out of neem wood, found floating in the Ganga and started worshipping at this spot. After his death, the idol of Chitteshwari was said to have remained unnoticed in the jungle, until a Tantric *sadhu* named Narasimha Brahmachari had a vision of the deity and thus had it reinstalled for worship in his house in 1586. The first temple was said to have been founded here in 1610 by Manohar Ghosh, a *zamindar* of the region, and the wooden idol is said to be one of the most ancient artefacts of Bengal.

The structure of the Chitteshwari temple, situated in the northern end of the city, has a strong Portuguese influence, like some of the other buildings in the area. Further north, there used to be a major Portuguese and Dutch trading centre before the British arrived.

The Siddheshwari Kali temple in Chitpur, also called the *dakaiter Kali*, occupies a historic location. It stands opposite the long destroyed structure of the nine-turreted temple, known in late 18th-century Calcutta, as the 'Black Pagoda' of Govindaram Mitra, named so after its founder's notoriety as an extortionist, or 'Black Zamindar'. Known by the images of the structure that survive in the *Views of Calcutta* of Thomas and William Daniell and Charles D'Oyly, the 'Black Pagoda' also has a special resonance in local memory as the place where the Nawab of Bengal, Siraj-ud-daulah, stopped to take the blessings of Goddess Kali in June 1756 before his victory over the British East India Company's forces at Fort William.

North Calcutta, stretching from Barabazar along the pilgrim route of Chitpur, towards Posta, Shobabazar, Kolutola, Manicktala and Sealdah, grew as a dense conglomerate of bazaars becoming the hub of Calcutta's Bengali and Marwari business aristocracy. Old coteries of Bengali, Marwari and north Indian *banias* and *mahajans* control the small shops and the wholesale retail trade of this area.

Maniktala, like Shobhabazar and Kolutola, developed as a more distinctly Bengali trading and residential neighbourhood, with many of the old markets here still retaining their earlier structures and stalls. This is a 120-year-old market owned by the Nan family.

Of particular visual delight is this fish stall in the market, where I saw the vendor weighing a large *hilsa* in the backdrop of a vibrantly painted image of Kali. For the Bengali, the *hilsa* remains the ultimate in gourmet cuisine.

Also at Maniktala is the Sreemani market. It exudes an old-world charm and familiarity that bonds vendors to an older generation of shoppers that has been coming here practically every morning.

One of the largest fruit markets in the city is the Fal-Patti at Machhuabazar, where I witnessed a banana auction in progress. The buyers babbled in an alien tongue while each bunch of bananas was individually paraded like an array of prospective brides!

Nearly a century-old shop, Gupta Perfumery is in one of the lanes of Shyambazar. The proprietor is from Benaras and sells *attar*, a perfume concentrate for different seasons or times of the day — such as *darbar* for winter, *kasturi* for summer or *shabnam* for the evening. The shop also specialises in varieties of *zarda* (chewing tobacco) which has different aromas like *zafranipati* and *muskipati*. The glass jars stored in rich Burmese wood cabinets seem steeped in a bygone era, a genteel past.

A typical sight at a wholesale market of the region is this onion, garlic and ginger bazaar at Posta. The owner, Mr. Das, sits at his *gaddi*, still using an antique wooden money box with a chain securing it to the ground, to hinder thieves. The *gaddi* is symbolic of the seat from which business is conducted, and has historically been associated with the trade of Marwari *banias* and *mahajans* in the city.

Of all the artisanal trades and quarters that mushroomed around Chitpur in the 19th century, the colony of *kumors*, clay modellers and idolmakers of Kumartuli, continues to survive. Spread across a cluster of crisscrossing alleys east of Baghbazar, Kumartuli feeds off its closeness to the river front and its ready supply of rich alluvial clay. The emergence of this skilled community of hereditary clay modellers was linked to the patronage of the *zamindari* households' Durga Pujas, and to the new trend of *barowari* and *sarbojanin pujas*, or community festivals of the 19th century. The five thousand or more idol makers who inhabit the colony, work in unbelievably dark, damp and cramped workshops, crafting clay gods and goddesses for the Vishwakarma, Ganapati, Lakshmi and Saraswati pujas. However, Durga with her entourage, and Kali, constitute their largest and most prolific output. The Kumartuli artisans today struggle to retain their traditional skills while asserting a new identity as 'artists'. They are increasingly seeking new channels for recognition of their work in the international arena. Changing artistic trends in puja designing now dominate the festival in the city. Yet, what still pervades is a sense of the traditional design repertoire handed down over the generations. Images of half-made, half-painted, unclothed idols, looming large out of the shacks of Kumartuli, are a ubiquitous part of the tourist's itinerary of Calcutta. As we see here, they continue to obsessively fascinate every old and new photographer of the city.

Through the tangle of lanes, images of unfinished clay idols greeted me at every turn. They were waiting to be clothed in the luminous colours of the painter's imagery. While I paused by the different works, I realised the skill and effort that goes into their making; a skill that is hereditary and untutored.

As the late morning light entered the lanes, the humdrum lives of the artisans were illuminated. A metal bucket, some steel utensils, a battered old cassette player and radio. They seemed to be basking in the comfort of their familiar space and in the warmth of the morning sun.

They are compelling, the tableaux of good and evil. Each year, as artisans mould their meanings, one hopes devotees decode them into their own lives.

The myriad limbs of the goddesses reflect mythical interpretations that are shaped by the human hand. Is the human hand too carved from pliant clay by Brahma?

An extremely daunting struggle for artisans is the retention of their traditional skills while exploring newer possibilities and asserting their identity as 'artists'. Today, many of them are seeking new avenues of exposure and publicity in an increasingly competitive market in India and abroad.

The dusty lanes of Kumartuli hum with the sculpting, moulding and painting of scores of fierce looking Kalis. The framework is made with bundles of hay bound together, then covered with clay from the bed of the Ganges. When dried and baked, the finished image is painted and decorated with sequins and ornate costumes. In this neighbourhood, every household seems to have a role to play in the making of gods.

The art comes from the land and its people. How magnificent their work and how humble their lives! These lanes are witness to a daily life, eked out in hardship. There is a gentle rhythm to their lives and a joy in simple pleasures. Sleeping in the sparse comfort of roughly made beds, waking to the business of another day of mixing clay and straw, moulding gods out of earth.

Leading out of Chitpur, in a bylane off the Nimtala Burning Ghat, one stumbles across a large, dilapidated temple, the Durgeswari Shiv Mandir, with an inscribed stone slab at the entrance bearing the date, 1794. Privately owned, the temple has its regular worshippers. Searching for one of the old *zamindari* houses in this vicinity, I was drawn by the soulful strains of a *bhajan* to this temple. When I entered, it took me a while to notice the four-foot high Shiva *linga* that stood inside, enveloped by a deep and still darkness. A short flight of stairs leads to a platform from which devotees offer flowers and prayers.

This was once a grand mansion. Many aristocratic homes of the Debs, Deys, Duttas, Lahas, Mitras or Mullicks had stood in the vicinity of Chitpur, defining the wealth and opulence of the 'Black Town', constructed as they were, in neo-classical, baroque, roccoco or Indian architectural styles.

The Chitpur Madrassa is one among many living remnants of the old Muslim heritage of this area. As I walked down Chitpur Road one morning, I glimpsed through a small gate, the huge courtyard of the Madrassa that drew me into its serene environs, away from the noise and bustle of the street. At one end, a few steps led to a spouting fountain; at the other end, sat a small group of children, ready for school. This solitary little girl sat under an arch, lost in thought.

When I looked out of the Nakhoda Mosque, I found this crumbling building, with its arched windows, staring at me balefully. Children at one of the windows caught my eye and lifted the tone of what looked otherwise like a brooding image.

In its serene resplendence, with marble verandas and staircases encircling a water tank, at Chitpur is the Nakhoda Masjid, Calcutta's largest and most well known mosque.

The Nakhoda Mosque's foundation stone was laid in September 1926, and took 16 years to complete. The ornate red sandstone and marble architecture was designed on the model of Emperor Akbar's mausoleum at Sikandra, with the main entrance replicating the Buland Darwaza at Fatehpur Sikri.

Calcutta has several ghats, or landing spots for boats, dotting the river bank. Some like the Chottalalki Ghat, that we see here, have colonial period architecture. Beside the Corinthian columns is a plaque dedicated to, "The memory of those pilgrims, mostly women, who perished with Sir John Lawrence in the cyclone of 25th May, 1887". While a few of the ghats have ferry services, carrying passengers to Howrah and back, most of them serve mainly as places of worship, where people come for a holy dip in the river. Here, a frail woman is making wicks for oil lamps.

Right: The Howrah Bridge over the Hooghly river is one of the most familiar and frequently photographed landmarks of the city. Replacing an earlier pontoon structure that had been built in 1874, the present 27,000-ton steel cantilever bridge came up as part of the war effort in 1943, linking the west bank of Calcutta to the city's main railway station at Howrah. Not surprisingly, it is said to be one of the busiest bridges in the world.

Overleaf: The Railway Quarters are near the Howrah Railway Station, the largest and second oldest station in India. The busy facade was graphically arresting, with its array of motley clothes drying in the colourful verandas. Like blobs of paint on an artist's palette.

Much of the quintessential character and fading grandeur of the 19th century 'City of Palaces' can still be seen in the architectural facades of the great, wealthy houses of north Calcutta. There is a lot that can be written on the ostentatious tastes, opulence and westernised lifestyles of a breed of Bengali absentee landlord and business agent, which made its fortunes working for the East India Company, and was lavished with titles and honours by the colonial masters. These new 'aristocrats' left their indelible mark on the elite culture of the 'Black Town' in the neo-classical and baroque mansions they constructed as their residences, filling them with European style furniture, statuary, porcelain and art works. Also, as major patrons of indigenous culture (of pujas, performances, dances and musical soirees), they were at the forefront of the Swadeshi fervour, setting new nationalist trends in lifestyle, sartorial tastes and ideology. The mansions of the Debs of Shobabazar, the Mullicks of Chorebagan, the Dattas of Hatkhola, the Lahas of Kolutola or the Tagores of Jorasanko and Pathuriaghata are today in varied states of preservation or disrepair. Yet, they continue to feature centrally in the commercial packaging of the 'heritage city'. The photographs revisit some of these grand Rajbaris of yesteryear, which once echoed with the rhythm of their owners' lives and their vibrant cultural engagements. They now resonate with a sense of loss, depletion and quiet nostalgia.

Durga Puja is celebrated every year with all the traditional regalia and resplendence in the two residences of the famous Shobabazar Deb family. Both houses, built across the street from each other between the period 1757-85, are attributed to Raja Nabakrishna Deb, the founder of the Shobabazar Rajbati. He ascended to power as a close business and political ally of the British in the years following the defeat of Siraj-ud-daulah in 1757. The house on 36 Raja Nabakrishna Street was built soon after the birth of his son.

Traditional Bengali homes are built with courtyards. The courtyard is a multi-purpose space used for drying pickles, clothes or a space to install the goddess, as in this Shobhabazar Rajbari. In the old days, it was a welcome space for itinerant performers who entertained families.

On Raja Nabakrishna Street, both the Shobabazar houses are today among the oldest and grandest of the architectural mansions of old Calcutta. They are widely known for their traditional and elaborate Durga Puja festivities which have begun to attract heritage tours in the city.

There were, it seems, three Laha mansions in the vicinities north of the famous Thanthania Kali temple at College Street. As with many old families, Durga Puja is a time for coming together and replaying traditional rituals. At the oldest of the three Laha Baris, an extended family of around 70 members still congregate for Durga Puja in the central courtyard of the house. I reached there just in time to witness the family raising hands in prayer, offering flowers to goddess Durga on *Ashtami*, the eighth morning of the festival.

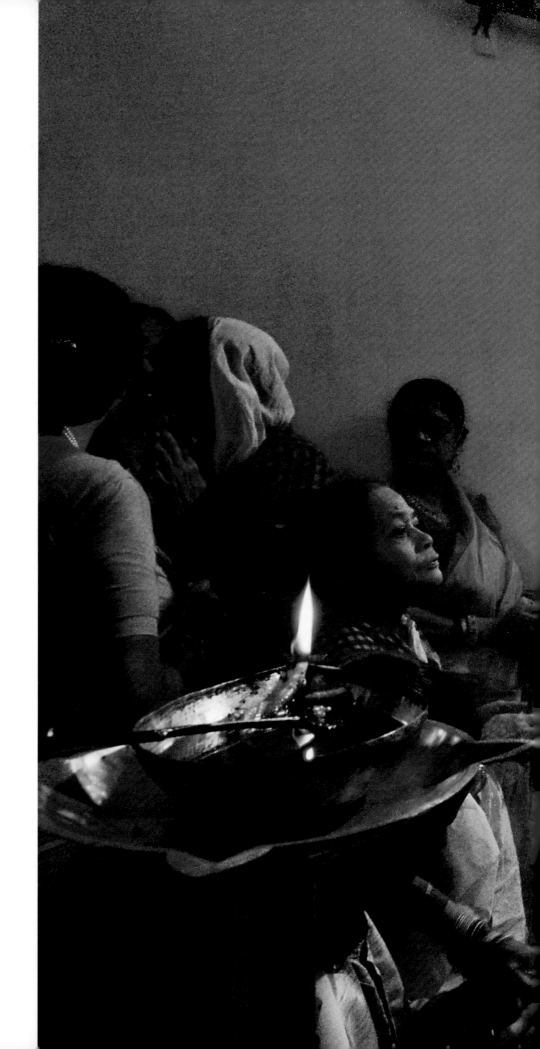

The *thakur ghar,* or prayer room, is an integral part of traditional Bengali homes, their scale and importance varying with the fortunes of different families. Bathed in the soothing green glow of lamps, this cavernous prayer room in a north Calcutta home, belongs to the Bhattacharyas on Beadon Street. After the evening prayers, a family member usually sings *kirtans.*

The Tagore Castle at 26 Prasanna Coomar Tagore Street was the residence of another member of the famed Tagore family. The design of the building was inspired by a turreted Scottish castle which Jatindra Mohan Tagore transported into the streets of Chitpur in 1896. Over decades now, the castle turrets and clock tower have disintegrated and the building has been leased to a Marwari businessman. It stands today as a forlorn reminder of the decline of a city's architectural heritage.

The celebrated writer and poet Rabindranath Tagore, India's Nobel laureate, is a household name and icon in Bengal. Called Gurudev, in the ultimate expression of respect, he is loved and valued not only by the highest echelons of Bengali society but has struck a chord at every level. A humble rickshaw-wallah offers his own whimsical appreciation of the poet by adorning his vehicle with Tagore's portrait.

College Street has long epitomised the image of a politically articulate and culturally dynamic city. The street took its name and character from the Hindu College that was founded here in 1817 and was laid out partially with funds from a lottery. The Hindu College later became the Presidency College, the oldest and most renowned institution of education in the country, hosting powerful ideological movements and political agitations — from the Derozian through the Swadeshi to the Naxalite era. Today, there is a cluster of the city's oldest educational institutions along its short stretch — from the Medical College, to the old campus of the Calcutta University to Hare School, Presidency College and Sanskrit College on Bankim Chatterjee Street. A large concentration of bookshops and Bengali publishing houses punctuate this street and one institution that has singularly represented and sustained its intellectual culture, is the Coffee House, tucked away in a building off the main road. An entire book could be written on this place and its legendary animated *addas*, (chats or discussions, in Bengali), that have, for decades, been at the core of the literary, artistic and political life of the city. Built in 1877, as the Albert Hall (after Prince Albert, the consort of Queen Victoria) as a venue for public gatherings and performances, the premises spanned two adjacent properties that were combined in 1916, to become the famed Coffee House in 1944. The 'Right of Admission Reserved' is a quaint notice that stands testimony to old times.

The whimsical 'Right of Admission Reserved' board stares you in the face at the entrance to the Coffee House like it is the portals of an exclusive club.

The Coffee House is abuzz as usual. A steady flow of its regular clientele, mostly students and academics, make it their favoured watering hole for endless discourses over a cup of "Infusion", a popular coffee concoction available in the menu. Interestingly, the waiters still wear old-fashioned, pleated fan-shaped hats, and the ancient, dangerously-dangling ceiling fans whirr quite precariously over one's heads.

Overleaf: College Street, with its rows of bookstalls, is a haven for students, academics and dedicated bibliophiles. The books, spilling on to the pavements, are quickly gone with a constant traffic of buyers.

Shops are stacked with books from floor to ceiling. An old man strains to read in the growing darkness, aided by the dim light from a pavement bookstall.

While the second-hand bookstalls offer little beyond textbooks, study guides, question papers and a smattering of bestsellers, some of the main Bengali and English publishers (like Rupa, Dasguptas, Chuckerbutty, Chattopadhyaya, the Deys, or the Sarat Book House), continue to hold sway here and stock the best, and often, rare literary and academic material.

The culture of the tea and coffee shop *addas* in the city is, however, one that goes back way beyond the time of the Coffee House on College Street. The Favourite Cabin on Beadon Street, seen above, is a tea house that has been there since 1918. A hub of the revolutionary nationalists, they gathered for their *cha-adda* in the back room, which had a passage of escape through the roof. When the police came, the tea shop owner tinkled his spoon against a cup as a secret code of alarm to the revolutionaries, who escaped, jumping from roof to roof across the crowded maze of houses in the neighbourhood.

Right through College Street, runs the tramline that is actually the lifeline of the city. The first tram rolled out way back in February 24, 1873. They were run on metre gauge and were horse-drawn between Sealdah and the Armenian Ghat. By the end of the 19th century, the entire system was converted to electric traction. Today, Calcutta is the only city in India where trams continue to wend their way through crowded streets even as there are rumblings of their closure.

During Durga Puja at College Square, the street is transformed into a spectacle of lights. For many decades now, the elaborate lighting of these tableaux has featured as a major attraction of the Puja *pandals*. The lights are designed and crafted by a small group of technicians from the suburban town of Chandannagar which has monopolised this trade for several decades. Like installation artworks, each display is an ingenious interpretation of a topical local or global event. Here, we see a recreation of a scene from an old and popular Bengali folktale collection, *Thakurmar Jhuli*.

At Bowbazar near College Street, a small temple houses a goddess known as *Phirangi* Kali or the foreign Kali, named after Anthony Kabiyal, Calcutta's early 19th-century poet-singer of Portuguese origin. His devotion for Kali and his becoming a *kabiyal*, composing poems for the goddess, is legendary. I first read about it in *Kalikatha via Bypass*, Alka Saraogi's novel, where she narrates how it was common for the British to take her blessings when they first arrived in Calcutta.

Idols or photo frames of gods and goddesses inhabit most of the shops, streets and gullies in the city. Turning a corner in a street, I found this tiny niche where an idol was adorned with the season's flowers.

The imposing Governor House was commissioned by Governor General Lord Wellesley in 1799 at a princely cost of Rs 15 lakhs to replace the old seat of power of the East India Company at Fort William. Designed by Charles Wyatt on the model of Kedleston Hall in England, it was meant to represent the most spectacular architectural symbol of the British Indian Empire, at a time when Calcutta was being offered up as the 'London of the East'. Renamed Raj Bhavan after Independence, and converted into the residence of the Governors of the state of West Bengal, this grand complex is the highlight of the colonial architectural heritage of the old Tank Square, or what subsequently has been known as Dalhousie Square and B.B.D. Bagh.

The Maidan was once the site of the old village of Gobindapur. A sprawling green belt, it was initially maintained by the British to provide an unrestricted field of fire from the adjacent Fort William. Considered now the lung of the city, it is a location for political rallies, cricket and football matches. Flanked by the Victoria Memorial and the Turf Club at one end, and the buildings of Chowringhee at the other, the Maidan is a welcome recreational space for Calcuttans.

The Victoria Memorial was built to commemorate the apogee of the British Empire in India. Lord Curzon, the then Viceroy, specified its classical style but its plans were actually laid down by the well known architect, Sir William Emerson, who blended the best of British and Mughal styles. Built with white makrana marble, the Prince of Wales laid the foundation stone of the Victoria Memorial in 1906, and it was inaugurated in 1921 in memory of Queen Victoria.

Overleaf: A revered icon of Bengal, the charismatic freedom fighter Netaji Subhash Chandra Bose, died mysteriously, but continues to live in the city's memories.

Calcutta has one of the oldest Anglo Indian populations in the country, which, in the past decades, has dwindled. Among the many surviving Anglo Indian pockets in the city, is Elliot Road in Central Calcutta. Like the adjacent Free School Street, (now renamed Mirza Ghalib Street), it carries fading resonances of the 'White Town', with its cluster of used books and record shops, a haven for the antiquarian collector. This laundry with its quirky homily continues to cater to a faithful clientele despite the onslaught of new, state-of-the-art services.

Just off the main thoroughfares of Chowringhee and Park Street is the Sir Stuart Hogg Market built in 1866. It is today called the New Market. This wonderful brick structure, with its clock tower, pointed arches and wooden sunshades, long stood its ground as one of Calcutta's most gracious and convivial market spaces.

This is a typical scene from the life of a small Bhabanipur shopkeeper, stamping the first page of his new *halkhata*, or account book, with a one rupee coin on *Poila Baishakh*, the first day of the Bengali New Year. It is a ritual performed by all Bengali traders on this day.

West Bengal has India's longest serving Left Front government. These flags and symbols have grown to be an intimate and integral feature of the city's visual signature. Here, it lends colour to an otherwise sombre residential building.

Calcutta is known for its frenzied football fans. Hundreds congregate during major matches between East Bengal and Mohun Bagan. On the walls of this residential house in Bhabanipur, political graffiti is replaced by cheerful murals of the World Cup football heroes of 2006. As in many Calcutta neighbourhoods, the mural was painted, most likely, at the behest of the local youth club. The name, 'Perfect Visual, that of a graphic studio on these premises, seems to complement the paintings.

KALIGHAT

Like Chitpur, Kalighat, named after the famous Kali temple that was erected here in 1809, is steeped in sacred legend and the history of the city. In the earliest documents, the region is referred to as Kalikshetra and was said to have been a special meeting point for both Shakta and Vaishnavite devotees, ascetics as well as householders. Whether or not the deity and the village Kalikata, that was once this region, lent its name to the city that was founded by the British, is still to be ascertained. What is known for certain, though, is that alongside the *zamindari* of the Sabarna Raychowdhurys at Barisha Behala, feeding off its patronage, Kalighat emerged as a thriving commercial and pilgrim zone that became the heart of the 'Black Town' of the south. The Kalighat of mid-19th-century Calcutta is today, world-famous for a particular genre of popular paintings that was produced and sold here by migrant village *patuas* to their pilgrim clientele. Brilliantly satirising the corrupt priests, foppish babus and lascivious courtesans who made up the life of the colonial city, these paintings document the degenerate religious and social worlds that had come to surround this holiest of holy temples. Traces of that world remain. They linger in a variety of ways in today's Kalighat — what with extortionate priests and the vast flow of funds that are associated with the temple, the bustling commerce that caters primarily to worshippers and their rituals, and, not least of all, the prostitution that is rampant throughout the dingy tenements of the bylanes.

Kali is a feminine form of the Sanskrit word *kala*, meaning 'Time'. It also means 'black'. Kali has therefore been translated variously as "She who is Time", "She who devours Time", "She who is the Mother of Time", "She who is black", and "She who is black Time". Kali is a goddess with a long and complex history in Hinduism. The earliest reference to her as a symbol of annihilation still has influence, while Tantric beliefs allude to her as the Ultimate Reality and Source of Being. Other interpretations conceive of Kali as a benevolent mother goddess.

The Lake Market dates back to the middle years of the 20th century, when it grew side by side with middleclass residential colonies that emerged all along the outskirts of the Dhakuria Lakes; and like these colonies, the market too made the Lake a part of its name. So, it came as even more of a surprise to chance upon this figure of a Bahurupee dressed like Kali, slinking away past the fruit and vegetable stalls. The *Bahurupees* are a dying breed of folk performers, who have young boys dressed up as various gods and goddesses enacting brief mythological skits. Encountered in village fairs or suburban trains, such figures are rare in the city today. The artist, K.G.Subramanyan, who would often see them in and around Santiniketan, talks about how, "between these village boys and the mythical stereotype a new reality is born, uniting the normal with the hieratic... the worldly with the unworldly".

I was riveted by the devout faces in this small Kali temple. Lost in prayer, the two women were oblivious to the cacophony on the street outside.

An innocuous sari flaps in the wind as it dries in the doorway of a house in the red light district of Kalighat, which is among the oldest of such areas in the city. It is also the most gritty; in its poverty, sleaze and grime. It is said that the first clients of these prostitutes were thugs and dacoits who came out of the surrounding jungles to loot the pilgrims, offering one-fifth of their booty to Kali, and squandering the rest on such pleasures. As is evident from the paintings and literature of 19th-century Calcutta, the pleasure houses of Kalighat were a great attraction for the Bengali *babus*. Remarkable is the fact, that the temple and the red light quarters — the so-called domains of piety and sin — have thrived for years in congenial co-existence.

The potato vendor sits blissfully munching a slice of watermelon, her eyes laughing, piercing through the camera. As vibrant as her sari and the smeared vermillion on her forehead, she seems to be enjoying life and its fruits to the fullest.

An overwhelming presence at the Kalighat temple are those seeking alms, largely women, who scrape together a living off the money and food that comes from the temple. There are said to exist at least 600 beggars at the temple. While most of them are unemployable, the more physically able beggars too are reluctant to accept jobs, believing they are an integral part of the temple.

Neighbouring Kalighat, is Chetla, where the area and its old temple site go back to the 18th century. Its character is no different from the many East Bengali refugee colonies of the post-Independence decades, where old and once opulent homes and curious little enterprises, such as this hair-cutting saloon, exist.

Walking once through Kalighat, I chanced upon this graphic image. An empty carton of eggs, placed right side up, a wok with something delicious cooking, and a spoon perched delicately on its side. The red chillies soaking in a bowl added an interesting synergy with the brick-red wall.

Calcutta, the once imperial capital, was embroiled in the victories that the British were scoring over the Nawabi regimes of Mysore and Avadh. Deposed and exiled in 1861 to Calcutta by the British, was Wajid Ali Shah, the last Nawab of Avadh, a poet and aesthete, under whom the Avadh culture reached its peak in refinement; from the visual and performing arts to etiquette, poetry and cuisine. He left his beloved Lucknow with 40,000 of his loyal followers and established Chota Lucknow in Metiabruz, a suburb in the southern fringe of Calcutta. The only memorial to the Nawab is the Imambara in Metiabruz where he lies buried.

The entrance to the Imambara, where a devotee rests awhile before his journey back home.

Left: Containers of herbs and potions line the shop of a *hakim*, a purveyor of traditional medicine, at the Imambara of Metiabruz. The *hakim's* ancestors migrated from Lucknow with the Nawab, 150 years ago. Age-old remedies like *zafrani tel* are still available to a small circle of loyal clients.

Above: Among the first of my images taken on Calcutta streets, is this play of green, ochre and white. The bunch of eggs hanging on the inside wall, framed by the bright green doors, caught my eye. They seemed so full, so pregnant with life.

If you judge people, you have no time to love them — Mother Teresa

Communities and People

A conglomerate of Eurasian trading communities — among them Parsis, Jews, Armenians and Chinese — contributed to the richly cosmopolitan character of the British city. Many of these groups had arrived centuries before the Europeans. The Armenians, for instance, had been part of a powerful silk-route trading network that had brought them to India as far back as the 11th century. They settled around Murshidabad and Chinsurah before the Armenian merchant community made its home in Calcutta. The Jewish traders too arrived via the route of Basra, Bombay and Surat to Calcutta at the end of the 18th century. Like the Jews, the first of the Parsi merchants, Dadabhoy Behramji Banaji and Seth Rustomji Cowasji Banaji, also moved to the colonial capital from Surat (between 1767 and 1812) to set up the city's most lucrative insurance and shipping businesses. The Chinese came, not as commercial magnates, but as small time peddlers, hawkers, shoemakers, tanners and plantation workers since the end of the 18th century, with the tide of migrants to the city noticeably swelling during the Chinese revolutions of 1912 and 1949. In all these instances, the common feature was the rapid diminishing of these communities over the years, now to the point of near extinction. A steady migration has taken them to Canada, the U.S., Australia and Hong Kong. These photographs serve as a memorial to these dying communities, capturing the few surviving traces of their lives in different pockets of the city.

Come rain or storm, the Fire Temple is where the older generation Parsis of Calcutta unfailingly converge to reaffirm their faith in Ahura Mazda, the Zoroastrian concept of divinity. Named after Rustomji Cowasjee Banaji, a philanthropist and shipping magnate, this Fire Temple was built in 1839 on Ezra Street.

The grandest monument to the long Armenian presence in the city is this Church of the Holy Nazareth. It is said to be one of the oldest Christian places of worship in Calcutta. The present church was erected through public subscription in 1724, replacing an earlier wooden chapel that stood a 100 yards south of this structure. Through the ornate grills, we see a service under way.

In 1990, the number of Armenians in the city, including students and refugees from Iran, was said to have reduced to just over two hundred. This Armenian home survives in the city as a rare vestige of this community's presence. The family houses seven dogs, all quickly banished as I came in. What remained was an overpowering canine smell. The green wall, the deep-hued tapestry of the floral curtain and the lady's skirt, her flaming hair, the little girl's red bangles, the slouched man — all came together in an unforgettable essay of images.

Offsprings of the old Indo-Eurasian population of India, the Anglo Indians were a distinct social community, contributing to a series of service ranks in British commercial firms and the Indian Railways. Here, a birthday celebration is in progress, where Mr Dias, has just turned 53. As he announces his 'old' age, his sister hugs him with affection. The Anglo Indians are a sociable and gracious community as they make me, a stranger in their midst, feel at home.

Most Jews of Calcutta trace their antecedents to 18th-century migrants from Baghdad, and through them, to the Babylonian Jews. There has been a great exodus out of the city over the years. Mr. Nahoum's confectionery store at New Market remains perhaps the only Jewish establishment in the city which is still in business. The fate of this establishment today is as uncertain as the historic structure and premises of New Market.

Chinese men gather at one of their regular social clubs at Tangra. In the post-Independence years, Tangra in East Calcutta, emerged as the new Chinatown, with a concentration of tanneries and restaurants, a Chinese school and two Chinese newspaper houses. Today, while the tanneries face closure, a conclave of restaurants has revitalised the area. It now draws a steady stream of the city's dining crowds.

The annual Chhat Puja in late autumn is a time when Biharis throng the streets of the city in long, drum-beating processions that make their way towards the river. Here, on the way to Babughat on the Hooghly, women devotees in red-bordered white saris prostrate themselves on the street, offering *dand pranam*, or their respects to god, as an essential part of these rituals.

The Marwaris have long since ceased to be known as merely a trading community, and are today acquiring a new profile in the city as professionals, industrial magnates, urban developers, philanthropists, and patrons of art and culture. At an opulent wedding, the fine clothes and jewellery of the Marwari women vie for attention with the ornate canopy.

These elite Bengali matriarchs and housewives (the archetypal *grihinis* or *ginnis* of the Bengali home), bedecked in the traditional red and white silk sari, reflect the leisured grace and orderliness of Durga Puja rituals performed in an aristocratic home in north Calcutta.

From cutting fruit and vegetables for *prasad* – an offering to the gods – to blowing conch shells, smearing themselves with vermillion powder and bidding a fond farewell to the goddess, the women of the house play a key role during Durga Puja.

Like fish, music, theatre, poetry and politics, sweets are an indispensable 'necessity' for a Bengali. Every *para* of the city boasts of one or more sweet shop, where a delectable variety is freshly made every day. Here, a neighbourhood granny eagerly shops for *telebhaja*, a popular batter-fried snack.

The narrow bylanes of Kalighat are full of shops that are as old and derelict as some of the people who hover around them. I spotted this frail and wizened man, taking a break from the day's chores above a small, dark tailor's shop.

The ancestors of this *doodhwallah* , the milkman at Chitpur, were migrants from Rajasthan. They were among the many small time Marwari traders who set up shop in these vicinities. Milk, which is thickened by slow cooking, is sold here by the metre! The faithful clientele are those who relish steaming milk with a scoop of *malai*, the thickened cream that forms on the surface of the milk, which is delicately ladled out into disposable clay cups.

The *dhakis*, drummers who flock to Calcutta from the surrounding villages of Bengal, play for various puja clubs and are essential to the spirit of the festival. The first beat of the *dhak* is like a clarion call, drumming excitement in the air. The *dhakis* are now much in demand across India and the globe, including select western museums, which have begun to host exhibitions of idol-making and festival rituals in their precincts. Unfortunately, the *dhakis* remain a distressingly poor community, subsisting on agricultural labour and seasonal occupation.

The streets of Bowbazar are home to a row of empty, inactive and worn out doctors' clinics — for whom there seems to be an acute dearth of patients.

Eclipsed from the sun outside, the tireless tailor is surrounded by spindles and cloth, his hands moving furiously to meet the contractor's deadline.

On the facing page, a watch repairer peers into my lens with curiosity. As curious is this shop from another era, with its walls full of antique clocks. Located on Vivekananda Road, the 'Perfect Watch Co.' as it is called, had begun its business in the 40s. A sign reads, "Favre Leuba Watches Sold Here", but essentially, it is now a watch repair shop.

The concept of the hand-drawn
rickshaw, it seems, arrived with the
first Chinese immigrants and soon
became one of Calcutta's many
modes of transport. In the congested
narrow alleys of the city, where
walking was a regular challenge,
Calcuttans used rickshaws as an
economical and efficient mode of
transport. The rickshaw-wallahs are
particular saviours in the monsoon
season, as they ply people through
flooded alleys. Inhumane as it
seems, to pull rickshaws manually,
this is the only source of livelihood
for these men who are mostly
migrants from neighbouring Bihar.
The state has announced a ban
on rickshaws from the city's streets
and their fate is in question.

In a city devoted to Kali and Durga, this Shaivite priest first caught my attention because of his dreadlocks. As I peered into his house, I noticed that half of it was devoted to a meticulously arranged prayer room. An unusual portrait of Shiva as a little boy, modelled after the child Krishna, adorned the wall, while the priest seated cross-legged, curiously mirrored the posture of the clay statue across him.

Mr. Shantimoy Bhattacharya is an antiquarian scholar with an encyclopedic memory that has served him well in his career as a city tour guide since the 60s. Shantimoy Babu's father's room is the central family altar, maintained as it was since his death in 1949. The family believes that the father's spirit is around; thus, offerings of his morning tea, the betel leaf after dinner, and his shaving kit and toothbrush, are laid out as a daily ritual.

Octogenarian artist Paritosh Sen is one of the founding members of the Progressive Art Movement of Bengal during the 1940s. As the city's well-known and seniormost painter, he continues to be prolific in his work and does not fail to grace most art events in the city with his acerbic and sprightly persona.

Nandikar, a leading theatre group in Calcutta, was founded in 1974. Gautam Haldar is one of its eminent actor-directors.

The theatre community in Calcutta evolved from early mythological plays to political engagements during the nationalist struggle to the classic theatre of Brecht, Ionesco and Chekov, and Bengal's famed Badal Sircar. No city in India lures as many serious theatre enthusiasts from diverse backgrounds as does Calcutta. Here, *Sojon Badeyar Ghat*, one of Nandikar's most celebrated theatre productions in recent years, holds a captive audience at the Academy of Fine Arts Theatre.

Actress, director, magazine editor and now television anchor, Aparna Sen has emerged in all these roles as one of Calcutta's unique celebrities. From being a talented child artiste in Satyajit Ray's films, she went on to become one of India's foremost film directors, evolving a special genre of serious English-language Indian cinema, like *36 Chowringhee Lane*, *Mr & Mrs Iyer*, and the recent *15 Park Aveneue*.

I first met Rita Dalmia when I went to shoot an old grandfather clock in her home for Alka Saraogi's book, *Sesh Kadambari*. She is one of the most remarkable Marwari women of her generation. Born to parents who were involved in Gandhji's Satyagraha Movement, she was adopted by her uncle, Raghunath Prasad Poddar. Unlike her natural parents, this was a wealthy business family connected to the British, where Ritaji was raised in luxury. She went on to become the first Marwari woman to graduate from Loreto House College in Calcutta and was awarded the prestigious Nagendranath Gold Medal by the Calcutta University.

Sheila Mukherjee, the daughter of Arun Kumar, the Baron Sinha of Raipur, wears her aristocratic lineage with grace. At 83, she is beautiful and regal. Widowed at the age of 27 with two small children, she defied her family and left for England to be trained under Madame Montessori. On her return, she established the Model KG Primary School, the first of its kind based on the Montessori method. Among the many successful students that she has schooled as toddlers is the eminent writer, Vikram Seth.

Minoti Das, or Meni Mashi as she is fondly called, relaxes in her ancestral home in Jangbazar. She is the direct descendant of Rani Rashmoni, an activist-*zamindar* of the early 19th century. In her legendary clash with the British, she had blocked the shipping trade on the Ganges and compelled them to abolish the tax imposed on fishing in the river, which had threatened the livelihood of poor fishermen. The British withdrew the penalty imposed on her in the face of public opposition and rioting in her support. She gave generously to charitable causes, including having the famous Kali temple built at Dakhshineshwar, where the saint, Shri Ramakrishna, attained divine enlightenment.

Aveek and Rakhi Sarkar, proprietors of the leading Calcutta daily, *Ananda Bazar Patrika*, are media barons and patrons of the art and literary life of the city. The Sarkars have an impressive collection of 19th- and 20th-century Bengal art. In the past decade, Rakhi Sarkar has come centre stage with the founding and running of CIMA (Centre for International Modern Art), an art gallery in the city. She is also poised to play a critical role in the setting up of the proposed Kolkata Museum of Modern Art.

Surendra Mullick of the aristocratic Mullick family resides in the 175-year-old Marble Palace. He was gracious in allowing me to take a portrait of him in his grand courtyard. But his reticence in being photographed is evident in his unease as he gestures to say, "Enough".

· ACKNOWLEDGEMENTS ·

I would like to thank Alka Saraogi for putting enough faith in an amateur to photograph her cover picture for her first novel, *Kalikatha via Bypass*, which went on to win the Sahitya Academy Award.

Thereon, the journey that started as an exhibition would not have been possible without encouragement from columnist Bunny Suraiya, curators Alka Pandey, Myna Bhagat and Tettei. And my thanks to Rajiv Sethi of the Asian Heritage Foundation, who asked me to look for the essence of Shiva on the streets of Mumbai for a book. He urged me always, to delve beneath a picture to reveal deeper layers. To Raghu Rai, for his critical appraisal, and S. Paul, whose feedback on my work has been invaluable. I would like to extend my thanks to Siddharth Pansari of the Crossword Book Store; a discussion with him was the genesis of this book. And Bina Sarkar Ellias, editor and publisher of Gallerie, who unwittingly opened new windows by asking me to do a photo feature on the different communities of Calcutta for her 'Two Bengals' issue.

Once I embarked on my journey, there were many who helped me. I would like to thank author Jaya Chaliha for sharing with me her knowledge of the city's communities. My teacher Mr. Raja Sarkar, for helping me understand my exposures better. Mr. Shantimoy Bhattacharya, our walking-talking encyclopedia on the city; I thank him for enlightening me with interesting anecdotes on his guided tours. I would like to extend my heartfelt thanks to the "we" in this project, my friend Baruna Bhattacharjee, an art historian with a keen, artistic eye. She has been with me since the beginning, making notes, lists and giving me valuable advice on the book, sharing anxiety to the point of spending sleepless nights!

To mamma and papa for giving me a happy and carefree childhood. To my brothers, sisters and our entire family for always being there for me, I love you all dearly. To my husband Ravi, and children Tushar and Vasvi, who are integral to all my experiences and with whom I share everything. Thank you for making life so beautiful. To Maa and Papaji for encouraging me and taking pride in my work.

My thanks to everyone in the photographs without whom the images would not be possible. A special mention to Sheila Mukherjee, Rita Dalmia, Parul Swaroop, Shantimoy Bhattacharjee, Minoti Das, Patsy Sharpe and Mr. Dias, Helen, Aparna Sen, Paritosh Sen, Aveek and Rakhi Sarkar and Mr. Mullick for inviting me into their homes. To Gautam Haldar of the Nandikar theatre company, for admitting me into the world of Bengali theatre; Mrs. Sonia John, principal of the Armenian School for letting us interact with the students; Mr. Gherda for shedding light on the Parsi community. Prince Nayyar Qudes, chairman, King of Oudh Trust and the manager, Syed Ali Mohammed of the Shahi Imambara, where the late and last Nawab of Oudh, Nawab Wajid Ali Shah lies buried. I would like to thank them for their warmth and hospitality. And to Shyam, for patiently driving me to whichever end of the city I asked him to. To Mashima and others who look after us with so much care, allowing me to work with an easy mind.

To my publisher, Ajay Mago of Om Books International, for having faith in my work. To my friend, Bina Sarkar Ellias, for taking deep and personal interest in editing and designing the book. To Nandini Bhaskaran, for her editorial contribution. And to Dr. Tapati Guha Thakurta for her immeasurable input in giving structure to my images, for the very informative introduction to the book and finally helping me with the detailed captions for each image.

And I thank all the others who contributed in big and little ways to make this work possible. Above all, to Calcutta, for being the way it is, and to God for giving me the ability to "see" and experience the beautiful world we live in.

THE PHOTOGRAPHER: LEENA KEJRIWAL

As a fine art photographer, Kejriwal is a licentiate member of the British Institute of Professional Photographers (LBIPP). She designed the book cover for Sahitya Akademi award-winning novel, *Kalikatha Via Bypass*, for Alka Saraogi, 1999 and created a series of fine art photographs for the Hyatt Regency in Calcutta and Mumbai in 2001. She has tried to capture the essence of spaces like Flury's, for the Apeejay group, and Shiva on the streets of Mumbai for a book conceptualised by Rajiv Sethi, besides life in a brothel for an NGO working against human trafficking. Her oeuvre includes work in villages around Calcutta, documenting craft-based cottage industries. She has had four solo shows depicting life on the streets, *Kalikatha*, 2002, *A Still Symphony*, 2003, *A Life of its Own*, 2003 and 2004. Kejriwal was the Brand Ambassador for Fuji Film, India in 2005 and an artist-in-residence in France (under the Indo French cultural exchange programme) in 2005-06. An exhibition of her works depicting life there is currently travelling in India.

FOREWORD: ALKA SARAOGI

Recipient of the Sahitya Akademi Award, 2001, for her first novel *Kalikatha via Bypass*, 1998, which has been translated into many languages in India and Europe. She has taught courses at the University of Cambridge, Turin, Naples. Heidelberg etc. Research projects on her book have been undertaken at various universities in India. Other novels by her are, *Shesh Kadambari*, 2001, published in English under the title, *Over to you Kadambari*, 2004 and *Koi Baat Nahin*, 2004. She has represented Indian writing at Belles Estranges (France, 2002), a seminar on collective memories in Indian writing (Turin, Italy 2003), a seminar by Mauritian Writers' Association (2004), the Berlin Literature Festival (Berlin, Germany 2004), Calendidonna, (Udine, Italy 2005), and the Frankfurt Book Fair 2005 and 2006. She has taught a course at the University of Venice on the Relationship between Hindi and Bengali Literature (2002). She was awarded with the 'Order of The Star of Italian Solidarity' in 2006.

ESSAY: DR. TAPATI GUHA THAKURTA

A professor of history at the Centre for Studies in Social Sciences, Calcutta, she has been educated in the city and has lived and worked here all her life, except for a period of four years (1984-1988), when she wrote her D.Phil. thesis at the University of Oxford. Trained as a historian, she later specialised in the history of modern Indian art and archaeology, and in the study of popular visual culture. Her two main books are, *The Making of a New 'Indian' Art; Artists, Aesthetics and Nationalism in Bengal* (Cambridge, Cambridge University Press, 1992) and *Monuments, Objects, Histories: Institutions of Art in Colonial and Postcolonial India* (New York: Columbia University Press, 2004). She also authored essays for select exhibition catalogues, including two booklets on exhibitions curated by her, *Visual Worlds of Modern Bengal: An Introduction to the Pictorial and Photographic Material in the Documentation Archive of the Centre for Studies in Social Sciences* (Seagull, 2002), and *The Aesthetics of the Popular Print: Lithographs and Oleographs from 19th and 20th century India* (Birla Academy of Art and Culture, 2006).

THE DESIGNER: BINA SARKAR ELLIAS

She is editor, designer and publisher of Gallerie, a global arts and ideas bookazine published from India. She is also a freelance writer, having written for national newspapers such as, *The Times of India Sunday Review*, columns in the *Indian Express* and *The Hindu*. She has edited, *Fifty Years of Contemporary Indian Art*, for the Mohile Parikh Centre for Visual Arts, Mumbai, 1997, and given and chaired discussions on art at art festivals in India and overseas. She has designed artist Jehangir Sabavala's catalogue for the 2002 show in Mumbai, Delhi and New York, artist Rekha Rodwittiya's catalogue, 2003, for the show in Mumbai, *Crossing Generations: diverge*, the fortieth anniversary catalogue for Gallery Chemould, Mumbai, 2004, and a book on artist Tyeb Mehta, *Svaraj* by Ramchandra Gandhi. She has designed and published an art book, *Chinthala Jagdish: Unmasked*, 2004, a book of poems, *Rain*, for Indian poet Sudeep Sen, 2005, Ayesha Talyerkhan's book of photographs, *Bombay Mumbai*, 2005 and American photographer, Waswo. X. Waswo's *India Poems: The Photographs*. Her chapbook of poems, *The Room* has been published by AarkArts, UK.

a maidan yawns
between the river
and a city

that once cradled
my uncertain youth
mapping new horizons
on old streets

housed by yellowed
crumbling walls
that spoke of
comfort in disrepair.

the trams trundled
into my head
in rhythm with Kafka

Camus and Sartre
as epiphanies
became searchlights
seeking other worlds

beyond the grid
of prescribed living.
and the bare feet
of a rickshaw-wallah

etched footprints
on my skin.

today,

the Victoria Memorial
still sits at the edge
of the drowsy maidan,

elegant, well-fed
and manicured,
presiding over a city

morphing from refined
decadence to plastic malls
and sweeping speedways

that snake into
my arteries with
asphalt, cement

and untold parables.

—Bina Sarkar Ellias

The city is
what it is
because its
citizens are
what they ar
— Plato
The city is
what it is
because its
citizens are
what they ar
— Plato
The city is
what it is
because its
citizens are
what they ar
— Plato
The city is
what it is
because its
citizens are
what they ar
— Plato
The city is
what it is

The city is
what it is
because its
citizens are
what they are
— Plato
The city is
what it is
because its
citizens are
what they are
— Plato
The city is
what it is
because its
citizens are
what they are
— Plato
The city is
what it is
because its
citizens are
what they are
— Plato
The city is
what it is